Van
HANDBOOK

JOIN OUR FACEBOOK GROUP FOR STORIES, TIPS,
TRICKS, WILD CAMPING, HIKING AND MORE

WILD CAMPING 101

ttps://www.facebook.com/groups/474823319998011/

THIS BOOK BELONGS TO

_____

MY CAMPER

My Camper is called: _____

The make and model is: _____

Current mileage is: _____

This is a picture of my camper.

Country's Visited.

DAILY LOG

Date:

Time:

Country:

Current area:

Weather:

Temprature:

Van's current mileage:

Today's plan:

DAILY PROMPTS

What are you most excited for today?

_____
_____
_____
_____

What are you going to try today that is new?

_____
_____
_____
_____

People you have met today or are going to meet.

_____
_____
_____
_____

Write 3 sentences decribing how you feel right now.

_____
_____
_____

An adventure a day keeps ~~the doctor away~~ you sane.

Notes and diary

Draw or Photographs.

Description.

_____
_____
_____
_____
_____
_____
_____
_____
_____
_____
_____
_____
_____
_____

DAILY LOG

Date:

Time:

Country:

Current area:

Weather:

Temprature:

Van's current mileage:

Today's plan:

DAILY PROMPTS

What are you most excited for today?

_____
_____
_____
_____

What are you going to try today that is new?

_____
_____
_____
_____

People you have met today or are going to meet.

_____
_____
_____
_____

Write 3 sentences decribing how you feel right now.

_____
_____
_____

An adventure a day keeps ~~the doctor away~~ you sane.

Notes and diary

Draw or Photographs.

Description.

_____
_____
_____
_____
_____
_____
_____
_____
_____
_____
_____
_____
_____
_____
_____

DAILY LOG

Date:

Time:

Country:

Current area:

Weather:

Temprature:

Van's current mileage:

Today's plan:

DAILY PROMPTS

What are you most excited for today?

_____

_____

_____

_____

What are you going to try today that is new?

_____

_____

_____

_____

People you have met today or are going to meet.

_____

_____

_____

_____

Write 3 sentences describing how you feel right now.

_____

_____

_____

An adventure a day keeps ~~the doctor away~~
you sane.

Notes and diary

Draw or Photographs.

Description.

_____
_____
_____
_____
_____
_____
_____
_____
_____
_____
_____
_____
_____
_____

DAILY LOG

Date:

Time:

Country:

Current area:

Weather:

Temprature:

Van's current mileage:

Today's plan:

DAILY PROMPTS

What are you most excited for today?

_____

_____

_____

What are you going to try today that is new?

_____

_____

_____

People you have met today or are going to meet.

_____

_____

_____

Write 3 sentences describing how you feel right now.

_____

_____

_____

An adventure a day keeps ~~the doctor away~~
you sane.

Notes and diary

Draw or Photographs.

Description.

_____
_____
_____
_____
_____
_____
_____
_____
_____
_____
_____
_____
_____
_____

DAILY LOG

Date:

Time:

Country:

Current area:

Weather:

Temprature:

Van's current mileage:

Today's plan:

DAILY PROMPTS

What are you most excited for today?

_____
_____
_____
_____

What are you going to try today that is new?

_____
_____
_____
_____

People you have met today or are going to meet.

_____
_____
_____
_____

Write 3 sentences decribing how you feel right now.

_____
_____
_____

An adventure a day keeps ~~the doctor away~~ you sane.

Notes and diary

Draw or Photographs.

Description.

_____
_____
_____
_____
_____
_____
_____
_____
_____
_____
_____
_____
_____
_____
_____

DAILY LOG

Date:

Time:

Country:

Current area:

Weather:

Temprature:

Van's current mileage:

Today's plan:

DAILY PROMPTS

What are you most excited for today?

_____
_____
_____
_____

What are you going to try today that is new?

_____
_____
_____
_____

People you have met today or are going to meet.

_____
_____
_____
_____

Write 3 sentences decribing how you feel right now.

_____
_____
_____

An adventure a day keeps ~~the doctor away~~
you sane.

Notes and diary

Draw or Photographs.

Description.

_____
_____
_____
_____
_____
_____
_____
_____
_____
_____
_____
_____
_____
_____
_____

DAILY LOG

Date:

Time:

Country:

Current area:

Weather:

Temprature:

Van's current mileage:

Today's plan:

DAILY PROMPTS

What are you most excited for today?

_____

_____

_____

_____

What are you going to try today that is new?

_____

_____

_____

_____

People you have met today or are going to meet.

_____

_____

_____

_____

Write 3 sentences decribing how you feel right now.

_____

_____

_____

_____

An adventure a day keeps ~~the doctor away~~ you sane.

Notes and diary

Draw or Photographs.

Description.

_____
_____
_____
_____
_____
_____
_____
_____
_____
_____
_____
_____
_____
_____

DAILY LOG

Date:

Time:

Country:

Current area:

Weather:

Temprature:

Van's current mileage:

Today's plan:

DAILY PROMPTS

What are you most excited for today?

_____

_____

_____

_____

What are you going to try today that is new?

_____

_____

_____

_____

People you have met today or are going to meet.

_____

_____

_____

_____

Write 3 sentences describing how you feel right now.

_____

_____

_____

_____

An adventure a day keeps ~~the doctor away~~
you sane.

Notes and diary

Draw or Photographs.

Description.

DAILY LOG

Date:

Time:

Country:

Current area:

Weather:

Temprature:

Van's current mileage:

Today's plan:

DAILY PROMPTS

What are you most excited for today?

_____

_____

_____

_____

What are you going to try today that is new?

_____

_____

_____

_____

People you have met today or are going to meet.

_____

_____

_____

_____

Write 3 sentences decribing how you feel right now.

_____

_____

_____

An adventure a day keeps ~~the doctor away~~
you sane.

Notes and diary

Draw or Photographs.

Description.

_____
_____
_____
_____
_____
_____
_____
_____
_____
_____
_____
_____
_____
_____

DAILY LOG

Date:

Time:

Country:

Current area:

Weather:

Temprature:

Van's current mileage:

Today's plan:

DAILY PROMPTS

What are you most excited for today?

_____
_____
_____
_____

What are you going to try today that is new?

_____
_____
_____
_____

People you have met today or are going to meet.

_____
_____
_____
_____

Write 3 sentences decribing how you feel right now.

_____
_____
_____

An adventure a day keeps ~~the doctor away~~
you sane.

Notes and diary

Draw or Photographs.

Description.
_____
_____
_____
_____
_____
_____
_____
_____
_____
_____
_____
_____
_____
_____
_____

DAILY LOG

Date:

Time:

Country:

Current area:

Weather:

Temprature:

Van's current mileage:

Today's plan:

DAILY PROMPTS

What are you most excited for today?

What are you going to try today that is new?

People you have met today or are going to meet.

Write 3 sentences decribing how you feel right now.

An adventure a day keeps ~~the doctor away~~ you sane.

Notes and diary

Draw or Photographs.

Description.

_____
_____
_____
_____
_____
_____
_____
_____
_____
_____
_____
_____
_____

DAILY LOG

Date:

Time:

Country:

Current area:

Weather:

Temprature:

Van's current mileage:

Today's plan:

DAILY PROMPTS

What are you most excited for today?

_____

_____

_____

_____

What are you going to try today that is new?

_____

_____

_____

_____

People you have met today or are going to meet.

_____

_____

_____

_____

Write 3 sentences decribing how you feel right now.

_____

_____

_____

_____

An adventure a day keeps ~~the doctor away~~
you sane.

Notes and diary

Draw or Photographs.

Description.

_____
_____
_____
_____
_____
_____
_____
_____
_____
_____
_____
_____
_____
_____

DAILY LOG

Date:

Time:

Country:

Current area:

Weather:

Temprature:

Van's current mileage:

Today's plan:

DAILY PROMPTS

What are you most excited for today?

_____

_____

_____

_____

What are you going to try today that is new?

_____

_____

_____

_____

People you have met today or are going to meet.

_____

_____

_____

_____

Write 3 sentences decribing how you feel right now.

_____

_____

_____

An adventure a day keeps ~~the doctor away~~
you sane.

Notes and diary

Draw or Photographs.

Description.

_____
_____
_____
_____
_____
_____
_____
_____
_____
_____
_____
_____
_____
_____
_____

DAILY LOG

Date:

Time:

Country:

Current area:

Weather:

Temprature:

Van's current mileage:

Today's plan:

DAILY PROMPTS

What are you most excited for today?

_____

_____

_____

What are you going to try today that is new?

_____

_____

_____

People you have met today or are going to meet.

_____

_____

_____

Write 3 sentences decribing how you feel right now.

_____

_____

_____

An adventure a day keeps ~~the doctor away~~
you sane.

Notes and diary

Draw or Photographs.

Description.

_____
_____
_____
_____
_____
_____
_____
_____
_____
_____
_____
_____
_____

DAILY LOG

Date:

Time:

Country:

Current area:

Weather:

Temprature:

Van's current mileage:

Today's plan:

DAILY PROMPTS

What are you most excited for today?

_____
_____
_____
_____

What are you going to try today that is new?

_____
_____
_____
_____

People you have met today or are going to meet.

_____
_____
_____
_____

Write 3 sentences describing how you feel right now.

_____
_____
_____

An adventure a day keeps ~~the doctor away~~
you sane.

Notes and diary

Draw or Photographs.

Description.

_____
_____
_____
_____
_____
_____
_____
_____
_____
_____
_____
_____
_____
_____
_____

DAILY LOG

Date:

Time:

Country:

Current area:

Weather:

Temprature:

Van's current mileage:

Today's plan:

DAILY PROMPTS

What are you most excited for today?

What are you going to try today that is new?

People you have met today or are going to meet.

Write 3 sentences describing how you feel right now.

An adventure a day keeps ~~the doctor away~~
you sane.

Notes and diary

Draw or Photographs.

Description.

_____
_____
_____
_____
_____
_____
_____
_____
_____
_____
_____
_____
_____
_____
_____
_____

DAILY LOG

Date:

Time:

Country:

Current area:

Weather:

Temprature:

Van's current mileage:

Today's plan:

DAILY PROMPTS

What are you most excited for today?

_____

_____

_____

What are you going to try today that is new?

_____

_____

_____

People you have met today or are going to meet.

_____

_____

_____

Write 3 sentences decribing how you feel right now.

_____

_____

_____

An adventure a day keeps ~~the doctor away~~
you sane.

Notes and diary

Draw or Photographs.

Description.

_____
_____
_____
_____
_____
_____
_____
_____
_____
_____
_____
_____
_____
_____

DAILY LOG

Date:

Time:

Country:

Current area:

Weather:

Temprature:

Van's current mileage:

Today's plan:

DAILY PROMPTS

What are you most excited for today?

_____

_____

_____

_____

What are you going to try today that is new?

_____

_____

_____

_____

People you have met today or are going to meet.

_____

_____

_____

_____

Write 3 sentences decribing how you feel right now.

_____

_____

_____

An adventure a day keeps ~~the doctor away~~
you sane.

Notes and diary

Draw or Photographs.

Description.

DAILY LOG

Date:

Time:

Country:

Current area:

Weather:

Temprature:

Van's current mileage:

Today's plan:

DAILY PROMPTS

What are you most excited for today?

_____

_____

_____

_____

What are you going to try today that is new?

_____

_____

_____

_____

People you have met today or are going to meet.

_____

_____

_____

_____

Write 3 sentences decribing how you feel right now.

_____

_____

_____

_____

An adventure a day keeps ~~the doctor away~~
you sane.

Notes and diary

Draw or Photographs.

Description.

_____
_____
_____
_____
_____
_____
_____
_____
_____
_____
_____
_____
_____
_____

DAILY LOG

Date:

Time:

Country:

Current area:

Weather:

Temprature:

Van's current mileage:

Today's plan:

DAILY PROMPTS

What are you most excited for today?

What are you going to try today that is new?

People you have met today or are going to meet.

Write 3 sentences decribing how you feel right now.

An adventure a day keeps ~~the doctor away~~
you sane.

Notes and diary

Draw or Photographs.

Description.

DAILY LOG

Date:

Time:

Country:

Current area:

Weather:

Temprature:

Van's current mileage:

Today's plan:

DAILY PROMPTS

What are you most excited for today?

_____

_____

_____

_____

What are you going to try today that is new?

_____

_____

_____

_____

People you have met today or are going to meet.

_____

_____

_____

_____

Write 3 sentences decribing how you feel right now.

_____

_____

_____

An adventure a day keeps ~~the doctor away~~ you sane.

Notes and diary

Draw or Photographs.

Description.

_____
_____
_____
_____
_____
_____
_____
_____
_____
_____
_____
_____
_____
_____

DAILY LOG

Date:

Time:

Country:

Current area:

Weather:

Temprature:

Van's current mileage:

Today's plan:

DAILY PROMPTS

What are you most excited for today?

_____

_____

_____

What are you going to try today that is new?

_____

_____

_____

People you have met today or are going to meet.

_____

_____

_____

Write 3 sentences decribing how you feel right now.

_____

_____

_____

An adventure a day keeps ~~the doctor away~~
you sane.

Notes and diary

Draw or Photographs.

Description.

_____
_____
_____
_____
_____
_____
_____
_____
_____
_____
_____
_____
_____
_____

DAILY LOG

Date:

Time:

Country:

Current area:

Weather:

Temprature:

Van's current mileage:

Today's plan:

DAILY PROMPTS

What are you most excited for today?

What are you going to try today that is new?

People you have met today or are going to meet.

Write 3 sentences decribing how you feel right now.

An adventure a day keeps ~~the doctor away~~ you sane.

Notes and diary

Draw or Photographs.

Description.

_____
_____
_____
_____
_____
_____
_____
_____
_____
_____
_____
_____
_____
_____

DAILY LOG

Date:

Time:

Country:

Current area:

Weather:

Temprature:

Van's current mileage:

Today's plan:

DAILY PROMPTS

What are you most excited for today?

_____
_____
_____
_____

What are you going to try today that is new?

_____
_____
_____
_____

People you have met today or are going to meet.

_____
_____
_____
_____

Write 3 sentences describing how you feel right now.

_____
_____
_____

An adventure a day keeps ~~the doctor away~~
you sane.

Notes and diary

Draw or Photographs.

Description.

_____
_____
_____
_____
_____
_____
_____
_____
_____
_____
_____
_____
_____
_____
_____

DAILY LOG

Date:

Time:

Country:

Current area:

Weather:

Temprature:

Van's current mileage:

Today's plan:

DAILY PROMPTS

What are you most excited for today?

_____
_____
_____

What are you going to try today that is new?

_____
_____
_____

People you have met today or are going to meet.

_____
_____
_____

Write 3 sentences describing how you feel right now.

_____
_____
_____

An adventure a day keeps ~~the doctor away~~
you sane.

Notes and diary

Draw or Photographs.

Description.

_____
_____
_____
_____
_____
_____
_____
_____
_____
_____
_____
_____
_____
_____

DAILY LOG

Date:

Time:

Country:

Current area:

Weather:

Temprature:

Van's current mileage:

Today's plan:

DAILY PROMPTS

What are you most excited for today?

What are you going to try today that is new?

People you have met today or are going to meet.

Write 3 sentences decribing how you feel right now.

An adventure a day keeps ~~the doctor away~~
you sane.

Notes and diary

Draw or Photographs.

Description.

_____
_____
_____
_____
_____
_____
_____
_____
_____
_____
_____
_____
_____
_____
_____

DAILY LOG

Date:

Time:

Country:

Current area:

Weather:

Temprature:

Van's current mileage:

Today's plan:

DAILY PROMPTS

What are you most excited for today?

_____
_____
_____
_____

What are you going to try today that is new?

_____
_____
_____
_____

People you have met today or are going to meet.

_____
_____
_____
_____

Write 3 sentences decribing how you feel right now.

_____
_____
_____

An adventure a day keeps ~~the doctor away~~
you sane.

Notes and diary

Draw or Photographs.

Description.

DAILY LOG

Date:

Time:

Country:

Current area:

Weather:

Temprature:

Van's current mileage:

Today's plan:

_____

_____

_____

_____

_____

_____

_____

_____

_____

_____

_____

_____

_____

_____

DAILY PROMPTS

What are you most excited for today?

_____
_____
_____
_____

What are you going to try today that is new?

_____
_____
_____
_____

People you have met today or are going to meet.

_____
_____
_____
_____

Write 3 sentences describing how you feel right now.

_____
_____
_____

An adventure a day keeps ~~the doctor away~~
you sane.

Notes and diary

Draw or Photographs.

Description.

DAILY LOG

Date:

Time:

Country:

Current area:

Weather:

Temprature:

Van's current mileage:

Today's plan:

DAILY PROMPTS

What are you most excited for today?

_____

_____

_____

What are you going to try today that is new?

_____

_____

_____

People you have met today or are going to meet.

_____

_____

_____

Write 3 sentences decribing how you feel right now.

_____

_____

_____

An adventure a day keeps ~~the doctor away~~ you sane.

Notes and diary

Draw or Photographs.

Description.

Van life
HANDBOOK

FOR DAILY WILD CAMPING AND VAN LIFE CONTENT
CHECK US OUT ON FACEBOOK.

WILD CAMPING 101
https://www.facebook.com/groups/474823319998011

Printed in Great Britain
by Amazon